FIGHTING FOR LIFE

Fighting for Life
Defending the Newborn's Right To Live

Melinda Delahoyde

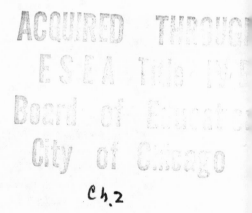
SERVANT BOOKS
Ann Arbor, Michigan

Cover design by The Cioni Artworks / Sarah Cioni
Cover photo by Jim Whitmer

Available from Servant Books, Box 8617, Ann Arbor,
 Michigan 48107

ISBN 0-89283-138-3

1 2 3 4 5 6 7 8 9 89 88 87 86 85 84

Printed in the United States of America

Contents

ONE

A Personal Perspective

FOR SEVERAL YEARS my husband and I have been speaking out on the issue of infanticide. In January, 1983, it became a very personal issue for us. That month our first child, William Arthur Delahoyde, was born. Will has Down's Syndrome. Now, with so many other parents, we are experiencing the joy and pain of having a special child.

We knew more about Down's Syndrome than most people. My husband Bill and I had been active in the pro-life movement for years and we knew that Down's Syndrome was certainly not a hopeless condition. Our experience, unlike that of so many other parents, has been one of constant love and support. Family, friends and doctors have rallied around us and worked to give Will the best possible care.

But no amount of knowledge or education can take away the pain and hurt of knowing that your own child is handicapped. We have grieved for the child Will will never be and for the son we will never have. I have had days of depression and I cannot claim that we are not concerned about the future. There is an extra pressure and anxiety as we watch Will grow. I find myself wondering how he will progress and what we can expect from him.

But this pain always comes in the midst of great joy. The joy is greater than any sadness we feel. Yes, raising a handicapped child presents special problems and difficulties, and I do not think that the pain you feel for your child ever totally disappears. But the joy and love that this child brings overshadows the pain. We had heard this from many parents of special children and now we have found it to be true ourselves. Will is the greatest joy of our lives.

Will is a happy, playful, busy little boy. As I am writing this he is rolling over, trying desperately to get hold of his favorite toy. He "talks" to anyone and everyone, bangs on his high chair with his spoon, and generally keeps me busy all day. At six months he is developing at his age level. Will's muscle tone is low and he is weaker than most children, but with exercise this will improve. We run through his exercises every day.

Bill and I are also learning a lot as parents. We haven't suddenly become "enlightened," but quiet insights come to us in bits and pieces as we live with Will. In those first weeks after Will was born our main reactions were shock and grief. Every day it seemed that some new part of this puzzle had to be understood, digested and taken into our lives. During those days God sustained us with a strong sense of his love and care. Yet, many times we could not see our way out of the dark cloud that engulfed us. It was months before we could begin to see the "bits and pieces" we were learning.

Bill and I are realizing what it means to love without expectations. We are learning a little more of what it means to love as Christ loves us. Both of us were raised in a generation that expects perfection. We had high expectations for ourselves. Ideas and education are a major part of our lives. We both have graduate degrees from Trinity Evangelical Divinity School in Chicago, and Bill also has a law degree. We have always believed that if you worked hard, achievement and success would follow. Yet, here is this wonderful little boy, the love of our lives, teaching us that success in the world's eyes is not important. Will probably will not go to college. His ability to reason abstractly will be very limited. His world will be much simpler than the one we know. We cannot have the same expectations for Will that we had for ourselves. And slowly we are learning that our expectations just do not matter.

We are beginning to understand that being different does not mean being less. There are certain things Will can never do, but this does not detract from who he is. Will is not less of a person because it will take him longer to walk and talk or because he will not be able to understand the intricacies of computer language.

I often talk with parents of other children with Down's Syndrome. Most of the time I doubt you would know from the conversation that our children are handicapped. We have not forgotten this fact. It is just that so much of our lives and theirs are wrapped up in "normal" baby things—what they eat, how they sleep and their favorite toys. Our children are children first and the fact that their abilities are limited does not change this in any way.

What is success? Bill and I thought we knew, but Will has changed our definition. Every new achievement is something we have all worked to accomplish. We just do not take anything for granted anymore. I honestly think that when Will walks we will be just as excited as the day Bill graduated from law school!

Whenever I think about success, I think of a young man named Mark. He is the nephew of a friend of my husband. Mark was born with a severe case of spina bifida. In his twenty-three years he has had multiple operations to correct various problems. Now he is learning to read and write, and he is the pride and joy of his family.

Mark's aunt was all smiles one day when she showed my husband a letter she received from her nephew. She had given him a simple book for a Christmas present. As a special present, Mark had written his aunt a letter. "Dear Aunt Sally" the letter began, and then, in the unsteady scrawl of a child just learning to write, Mark had copied a page of the book our friend had given him. It had taken him hours to do. As his aunt told us, "He always does his very best." Mark is twenty-three years old and he is just learning to write. Mark is a success!

He is a great encouragement to me when I think about Will and our future.

Our lives will forever be different because of Will. Handicaps do not go away. When you raise a special child you walk down a different road in life—an often difficult and unknown road. But with the difficulties comes a new freedom to love and to give to others. Bill and I have found that freedom in our lives since Will was born. It is the freedom to reach out and share ourselves with those around us. It is a freedom from trying to live up to expectations about ourselves that just do not matter. It is the freedom to share our feelings and to reach out to those who are also experiencing pain and suffering. Will has opened up those feelings in us.

Learning that your child is not "normal" is not easy. But neither are so many other of life's situations. God uses the tough times, the broken heart, the bruised body, the hurts and pains to show us more of himself and to deepen our ability to love. We are truly blessed to have Will in our lives. He has brought more joy and happiness to us than we could ever have hoped. We would not trade him or our situation with anyone else in the world.

My experience as the mother of a handicapped child has intensified my concern over infanticide. Will was lucky. Babies like him do not always leave the hospital alive in the United States. I had been speaking out about infanticide for years before Will was born. Now, no longer viewing it simply as an "issue" but as an intensely personal experience, I can see infanticide from the inside.

TWO

Infanticide: Down the Slippery Slope

ON APRIL 9, 1982, a baby boy known only as Baby Doe was born in Bloomington Hospital in Bloomington, Indiana. The baby, the parents' third child, was diagnosed at birth as having Down's Syndrome. He also had a badly formed esophagus which required an immediate operation. Without this operation, which is successful more than 90 percent of the time, the baby would be unable to digest nourishment and would die.

Pediatricians consulting on the case advised immediate surgery. But the parents, after consulting with their obstetrician, refused the surgery for their infant. They knew this would mean death for him, but they were convinced their child, born with Down's Syndrome, had no chance for a meaningful human life. Their decision was final.

Lawyers for the baby frantically took the case to the Indiana courts, hoping to convince judges that the parents were wrong and this child deserved a chance to live. Two state courts, including the Indiana Supreme Court, refused their petition and left the child's fate in the parents' hands.

As one of the judges said, the parents "have the right to choose a medically recommended course of treatment for their child in the present circumstances."[1]

As Baby Doe's lawyers raced against the clock, pediatricians in the Bloomington hospital tried to convince the parents to let them operate. The baby, now starving, had been transferred to a private room on another floor because the nurses in the newborn nursery could not stand to hear the cries of this dying newborn child.

As Baby Doe's lawyers boarded a plane to take their case to the U.S. Supreme Court, doctors in the hospital made one final attempt to save this child. They raced to the baby's room with an IV and equipment to force feed Baby Doe. Their attempts were too late. Upon entering the child's room this is what they found.

> Baby Doe's shrunken thin little body with dry cyanotic skin, extremely dehydrated, breathing shallowly and irregularly, lay passively on fresh hospital linens. Blood was running from a mouth too dry to close. Death by starvation was near. Too late for fluids. Too late for surgery. Too late for justice.[2]

Baby Doe's death was a clearcut case of infanticide. Infanticide is the killing of an infant by direct or indirect means. Baby Doe was killed by the intentional neglect of his parents and doctors at the hospital. A child who had every chance to live was killed by those who thought his life was not worth living.

Many Americans heard the word "infanticide" for the first time in connection with the Baby Doe case. Yet for years doctors had been aiding the deaths of handicapped newborn babies—babies who were not born dying, but who needed help to live. Baby Doe was only one of hundreds, perhaps thousands, of children who never survived the newborn nursery.

In June of 1981 the *Hartford Courant* ran an extensive series of articles on infanticide. At Yale-New Haven Hospital reporters found cases of parents giving lethal overdoses of morphine or phenobarbital to their newborn children.

One couple (who did not have their baby at Yale-New Haven) whose child was treated against their will, told of killing their baby at home. They began a daily increase in the dose of anti-convulsive sedative administered to their child. Six days later their baby died. The couple's doctor was not aware of the action, but later affirmed the parents' decision. In his opinion, the child was "socially dead and would never come alive." In the parents' words, "We did it out of love."

In England, Dr. Hugh Jolly frankly admits that the non-treatment of handicapped children is part of the medical program at London's Charing Cross Hospital. If doctors and parents decide the baby might not enjoy a good quality of life, the child is put on a "water only" diet, with sedatives if necessary. Dr. Jolly does not like to refer to this as killing because of the feelings of the hospital staff. Instead he calls it "conservative treatment."

One nurse, talking to a reporter in 1983, described her own experience of infanticide of babies with Down's Syndrome:

> The doctor would see the baby's head coming out through the birth canal, realize it had Down's Syndrome, and signal us to let it die. The mother's legs would be up so she couldn't see what was going on. We would get a little wave of the doctor's hand—a signal to us not to use suction on the baby. [Then] they'd say to the mother, "we're just going to give you something to relax you" and the next minute she'd be unconscious. When she came around, they'd say the baby had died on delivery.[3]

Neglect of handicapped infants is not limited to those with Down's Syndrome. Baby Jane Doe was born on October 11, 1983, in Stonybrook Hospital in New York. Baby Jane had spina bifida. Sometime during the first few weeks of her development in the womb, her spinal cord had failed to form properly. At birth she had an open lesion on her lower back where the spinal cord and overlapping skin had failed to close.

In addition to her spinal condition Baby Jane had also developed hydrocephalus, an accumulation of fluid on the brain often associated with spina bifida.

The girl needed immediate surgery. The wound on her back had to be closed to prevent infection and possible mental retardation. A device known as a shunt needed to be surgically implanted in her brain to drain excess fluid and to prevent further building up of pressure. Both of these procedures had become routine treatment for an infant with Baby Jane's condition.

At first her parents gave their permission for surgery. But after consultation with a doctor at Stonybrook, they withdrew their consent and decided against any surgery for their daughter. They chose a more "conservative" treatment—a regimen of antibotics to fight the infections that would invade Baby Jane's body. Without surgery, one doctor told them, their little girl would die within two years.

At this point several people became concerned that Baby Jane was not receiving proper care. One New York attorney filed suit in court claiming that the child was the victim of discrimination—that she had been denied normal medical care simply because she was handicapped.

The network media picked up the case and reported on the "agonizing decision" that faced Baby Jane's parents. Many early press accounts said the child would never achieve "meaningful social interaction" with the outside world and that she would live only twenty years of intense pain in a severely retarded state of mind if she had the surgery. The general consensus of the media was that her parents had acted rightly in denying her the surgery.

Yet others were not convinced. The federal government petitioned the New York courts to obtain Baby Jane's medical records so it could look for any evidence of discrimination. Parents of children with spina bifida practically begged Baby Jane's parents to consent to surgery for their baby. Others volunteered to adopt the baby girl.

It was then that the real truth about Baby Jane began to

emerge. While the press had spoken of a severely retarded, bedridden "vegetable," they did not mention other medical viewpoints and contradictions in the court testimony of physicians. One doctor predicted that Baby Jane would be unable to leave her bed, but later testified that she would probably walk with braces. Other doctors, experts in the treatment of spina bifida, disputed the twenty-year life expectancy. They said many such babies have a normal life expectancy if aggressive treatment were provided. Newspaper stories suggested that Baby Jane would almost certainly be severely retarded because of her small head size. But physicians were not sure that the head was small at all and thought Baby Jane might not have *any* retardation.

Dr. David McLone is the Chairman of Pediatric Neurosurgery of the spina bifida clinic at Children's Memorial Hospital in Chicago. He commented that in his best judgment, if Baby Jane had been given aggressive treatment at birth and if she had been in the hands of doctors at their clinic, he would have predicted normal intelligence and that she would have been able to walk with assistance.

The medical testimony had shown that Baby Jane may well have been the victim of discrimination. It is important to note that the operation Baby Jane needed was not considered "extraordinary" treatment. These procedures—the operation to close the back lesion and the insertion of the shunt—are *normal* medical treatments for an infant with spina bifida. Attorney Paige Cunningham had this to say about the Baby Jane case:

> Not only have they said that the child is being medically neglected as no otherwise nondisabled child would be neglected, they admit she is being treated differently than children with problems exactly like hers are normally treated—all because doctors and the courts deem that ... the parents have a private right to preside over the death of an unwanted child.[4]

Infanticide and Abortion

How do things like this happen? How can it be that those members of the human family who need our special help and care should instead be left to die? How did we arrive at the place in our society where we starve some newborn babies to death? How can it be that some handicapped babies are denied routine medical care simply because they are handicapped?

Events do not happen in a vacuum; infanticide did not just suddenly appear on the American scene. Ideas have consequences, and ideas about the low value of human life took root in our culture long before Infant Doe was killed in Bloomington. Infanticide is the logical conclusion of a mindset that casually allows the destruction of more than 1.6 million unborn children every year.

Abortion leads to infanticide. In 1973 the Supreme Court told us that some human lives, the unborn, were not worth protecting under the law. Some human beings can be destroyed at the mother's word. But if the unborn can be destroyed because they are unplanned or imperfect, then why not destroy a newborn child for the very same reasons. After all, what is the difference between taking a human life three days before birth and taking that same life three days after birth? There is no real difference except that before birth we call it "abortion" and after birth, "infanticide."

If we can say that an unborn child is not really a person because he does not possess certain human qualities, then why can't we say a newborn child is not really human if the child is handicapped? After all a handicapped infant may lack some of the qualities we call "human." Why not simply define them as "sub-humans," like we did the unborn, and then simply leave them to die without qualms because we aren't killing a "human being?"

Medical ethicists like Joseph Fletcher have seen the logical link between abortion and infanticide for years. In Fletcher's eyes, "It is reasonable to describe infanticide as a post-natal abortion."[5]

Another ethicist, Milton Heifetz, was equally clear.

> Is life at birth more significant than at the second, fourth, or sixth month of pregnancy? It is not. True it is closer to gaining the attributes of man, but, as yet, it has only the potential for those qualities. If this difference is true for the normal newborn, how much less significant is it for the newborn who doesn't even have this potential?[6]

This connection between abortion and infanticide was made clear to me several years ago when I was a graduate student researching an article on abortion for a philosophy professor. I had read many articles by philosophers who would be labelled "pro-abortion." Philosophers are always ready to draw out the logical and ethical consequences of an idea they hold. Philosophers can tell us what's coming because they usually articulate ideas long before they take hold in our culture as a whole.

The philosophers I read clearly understood the consequences of the pro-abortion position. They were quick to point out that abortion would logically lead to infanticide. All of the arguments put forth to justify abortion also justified killing a newborn baby. Of course, they were equally quick to point out they didn't think infanticide would ever happen in this country because socially speaking, it was unthinkable.

But they were wrong. Infanticide is happening today. As theologian Francis Schaeffer says, "the unthinkable becomes thinkable." Years ago no one would have believed that starvation of newborn babies would become a treatment option in American hospitals. People generally assumed, "It can't happen here." But when certain ideas are put in place, certain consequences necessarily follow. The idea that some human lives are worthless has been around a long time and it was enshrined in Constitutional law by the Supreme Court.

Now we see the fruit of that idea in the deaths of handicapped newborn babies. When we ask ourselves "how did we get there" we must look back to abortion for part of the answer.

A New Medical Ethic

Nowhere is this progression from abortion to infanticide more clearly illustrated than in the words of doctors themselves. In 1973, *California Medicine,* a leading medical journal, published their now-famous editorial about abortion and medical ethics.[7] That editorial plainly acknowledged that abortion was the taking of a human life and noted that our society could justify this killing only by calling it something else. It concluded that society takes such pains to justify the killing because we had accepted the idea that some human lives weren't worth living.

Ten years later, *Pediatrics,* the leading journal for pediatricians, published a similar commentary. This time the subject was newborn human life and medical ethics. In the author's words:

> If we compare a severely defective human infant with a dog or a pig...we will often find the nonhuman to have superior capacities . . . Only the fact that the defective infant is a member of the species *Homo sapiens* leads it to be treated differently from the dog or pig. But species membership alone is not relevant.... If we can put aside the obsolete and erroneous notion of the sanctity of all human life, we may start to look at human life as it really is: at the quality of life that each human being has or can attain.[8]

In other words, human life isn't special. We should compare our children to pigs and dogs and whoever comes out ahead is allowed to survive. We have moved one step further in the devaluation of human life. Ten years ago the quality of life world view gave us abortion on demand. Today that same mind-set brings us infanticide.

But how did this happen in the medical profession? How can it be that respectable doctors now tell parents that their newborn baby is better off dead than alive. How did we arrive at the point where doctors ask themselves not "How do I treat?" but "Should I treat?"

Attitudes change long before that change reveals itself in an actual event. The attitude of the medical profession toward human life has been changing for more than a decade. In 1973, the same year that abortion was legalized, Drs. Raymond S. Duff and A.G.M. Campbell, two doctors at Yale-New Haven hospital, detailed the reasons for forty-three infant deaths in the newborn nursery in which they practiced. All of these deaths were caused by decisions to withhold or discontinue treatment. Some of these children were literally "born dying" and could not be treated at all. But many had every chance to live. These children had beneficial treatments withdrawn. Several had Down's Syndrome, and others had spina bifida. But because the babies were handicapped, doctors advised parents against treatment. The doctors based their decisions not on their best medical judgments but on "social" factors like financial responsibilities and the emotional state of the family. In the authors' words:

> We believe the burden of decision making must be borne by families and their professional advisors because they are most familiar with the respective situations. Since families primarily must live with and are most affected by the decisions, it therefore appears that society and health professionals should provide only general guidelines for decision making.[9]

Drs. Duff and Campbell were the first to tell us that infanticide is taking place in the newborn nursery. But they also told us that the "quality of life" attitude had taken hold in the newborn nursery. Handicapped babies were being chosen for death, not because they could not live, but because others judged their lives to be worthless.

Several years after Duff and Campbell wrote, a distinguished group of doctors and health care professionals gathered for a conference on biomedical ethics in Sonoma, California. A questionnaire passed out at the conference asked them to answer the following question: Would it ever be right to intervene to directly kill a self-sustaining infant? It was not a question of withdrawing a respirator or some other means of sustaining life. The question concerned infants who were living independently of machines or breathing devices. Seventeen out of twenty respondents answered yes, they could forsee circumstances in which they would kill a child. Some of these people indicated they themselves could not kill the baby, but they certainly would not condemn someone else who would.

It was during these years that Johns Hopkins Hospital produced a film entitled *Who Shall Live*. The documentary detailed the death by starvation of an infant boy born with Down's Syndrome in the university hospital. The case was strikingly similar to the death of Baby Doe. The baby required a routine operation to correct an intestinal blockage. Here again, the parents chose starvation for their son. A sign was placed over the crib reading, "Do not feed." Fifteen days later the baby died.

The documentary of this death is shown in medical schools across the country. It is used to show future doctors how to handle a difficult ethical situation.

The extent of the medical profession's shift from a sanctity of life perspective to a quality of life value system was shown in a national poll in 1977 of the attitudes of pediatricians and pediatric surgeons. Almost seventy-seven percent of pediatric surgeons and sixty percent of pediatricians responding said they would go along with a parent's decision to refuse surgery for a child with an intestinal obstruction if that child also had Down's Syndrome. Almost twenty-four percent would encourage parents to refuse their consent for treatment. Less than four percent would go to court, against the parents' wishes, to obtain an order to treat the child. In cases where parents and physicians had agreed to let a baby die, almost sixty-four percent of the pediatric surgeons would hasten the process by stopping all nourishment and supportive care for the baby.[10]

We need to understand what we are talking about here. Three fourths of the nation's pediatric surgeons who responded would refuse a life-saving operation for a handicapped child. This is not a child born dying, but rather a child who has every chance for a life filled with hope and love. This is a child who will most likely be able to read, write, and may be able to take a job. Only a tiny percentage of those surgeons surveyed (3.4 percent) would try to obtain a court order to treat the baby.

The Duff-Campbell article, the Sonoma Conference questionnaire, and the Johns Hopkins baby, have been instrumental in changing the medical community's view on the handicapped infant. Those who want us to accept a quality of life value system have been working for at least a decade to convince us and their medical colleagues that killing is often the most compassionate course of action. In many different ways, through many different channels, the pro-infanticide forces have effectively communicated their message to the medical profession.

The death of Baby Doe took many Americans by surprise, but that event could never have taken place if the groundwork had not been laid years before in the minds of doctors and nurses. How did we get there? Much of the answer lies in the quality of life view that so many in the medical profession have embraced.

Infanticide is now a feature of American life. Some handicapped babies are being denied treatment. Some are literally starved to death in the name of "love" and "compassion." Doctors who have been devoted to the care and healing of our sick are now becoming death dealers for those whose lives are not "worthy to be lived." A society once known for its loving concern for its most helpless members now kills its unborn and even newborn children.

Many said, "It can't happen here." They were wrong. It is

happening here. The death of our handicapped babies moves us several steps further down on the slippery slope of planned death for all those who don't measure up to our always changing standards of what it means to be a person.

THREE

"Complexity" and Other Issues

MISCONCEPTIONS AND DISTORTIONS continue to surround the issue of infanticide even as it basks in the glare of sudden publicity. Some medical decisions about handicapped infants are genuinely complex. Not every decision to withhold or withdraw treatment from a critically ill child is infanticide.

Indeed, the medical complexity of a particular child's situation can keep us from a clear overview of exactly what is happening in American hospitals. Pro-infanticide advocates often dwell on the complexity of a particular case in order to introduce the idea that the issue is so complex that there are *no* clear-cut principles to guide our decision-makers. In fact, there are clear guidelines we must follow to protect innocent human lives. Let's clarify the issue.

Many people do not understand the difference between committing infanticide and choosing not to prolong the death of an infant. Doctors have always made choices to discontinue a useless treatment or not to begin a treatment that will not benefit the patient. If no known medical treatment will improve a handicapped child's chances for life, then no treatment should be given. If the child is born with so many anomalies that the case is *medically* hopeless, and there is no

17

prognosis for recovery and future life, then again treatment is not required. In short, doctors are not obligated to prolong the death process by providing useless treatment. Doctors who do not treat in these situations are not committing infanticide.

Dr. C. Everett Koop, our nation's Surgeon General and a leading pediatric surgeon, has written of his own experiences with terminally ill youngsters. He writes:

> I happen to belive that the terminal patient . . . for example should be permitted to die as quietly and in a dignified manner as possible rather than to use every conceivable combination of chemotherapeutic agents for the prolongation of life without alleviation of the disease.[1]

This is the morally correct way to treat a dying child. Unnecessary treatment is not demanded. To refuse to give useless treatment is a truly compassionate form of care for a dying patient. By contrast, victims of infanticide are infants who are *not* dying but are nevertheless refused care. There is an accepted medical treatment that can be given these children, but they are denied the treatment only because they are handicapped.

This is the heart of the infanticide debate. No one is demanding that a baby be kept alive at all costs when the child has no chance for life. No one is telling doctors to put aside their best medical judgments in order to give a child a treatment they think is useless. The problem comes when physicians stray outside their field of expertise—medicine—and make value judgments about the *worth* of a child's life that have nothing to do with the baby's medical condition. Value judgments, not medical judgments, led to the death of children like Baby Doe in Bloomington.

Advocates of infanticide claim that neonatal treatment situations are "too complex" for anyone to judge and that only the child's doctor and parents can make a life or death decision.

This is seldom true. Let's look again at two of the most publicized infanticide cases, Baby Doe in Bloomington and the Johns Hopkins baby.

In both these cases the children were born with Down's Syndrome. Down's Syndrome is not a life-threatening condition (we will discuss Down's Syndrome in more datail later). Both the Bloomington and Hopkins babies had every chance to live, but, as is often the case with children with Down's Syndrome, they needed an operation to correct blockages that kept them from ingesting nourishment. The success rate for these operations, which are routinely performed, is more than 95 percent. No one doubts that both these infant boys would have had immediate surgery if they had not been born with Down's Syndrome. But because they were handicapped, they did not have the operations and were left to starve to death.

Those who supported Baby Doe's parents' decision not to treat their child maintained that the situation was too complicated to judge. In their opinion the child was "severely retarded" and had only a minimal chance of survival.

But what is so complicated about this particular case? The child needed an operation and his parents refused. As a result the baby died. The best *medical* judgment in both cases was that the babies should have had the operation. But the decisions about these children were based on *social* judgments about the baby's quality of life. What makes these cases "complex" is the introduction of value judgments about the baby's quality of life.

These decisions become much easier when we begin with the idea that every human life has value. Children deserve to live, and they should receive available and appropriate treatments. The situation becomes "complex" only when we begin weighing the value of the child's life against other factors like the parents' preferences and the financial cost of caring for the baby. "Complexity" is often a smokescreen to hide the kind of thinking going on here. The baby's right to life becomes only one of many rights that must be "weighed and measured."

Sometimes the right to life comes out on top and the baby lives. Sometimes not.

There is another example worth noting. In Illinois, in 1982, a baby boy named Kevin was born with spina bifida—an opening in the spine that needed to be surgically closed. The child's parents refused surgery. Thanks to the determination of several Chicago women, the case became public and the federal government became involved. The baby boy was transferred to a children's hospital in Chicago and the operation was performed. Later Kevin was adopted by an Illinois couple and given the love, care and attention that only a family can provide.

Today Kevin is over one year old. He said his first word at seven months. Kevin stands with the help of leg braces and as far as the family can see there are no signs of mental retardation. Here again is a situation that many would have labelled "too complex to judge." Many said Kevin's life would be full of pain and suffering and his parents should be allowed to let him die. But this case was not too complex. Kevin was merely provided with the care he needed. Today he is growing and developing like any other child.

Let's look at a more difficult case. In 1981 Siamese twins were born to a doctor and his wife in Danville, Illinois. The twins, Jeff and Scott Mueller, were joined at the waist and shared several organs. A nurse testified at a preliminary hearing that at their birth their father ordered no oxygen be given the babies and also insisted that they receive no food or water. The twins were taken to the nursery and left to starve.

Jeff and Scott would have died had it not been for an anonymous call which informed the Department of Child and Family Services that the babies were being neglected. That call resulted in an indictment for attempted murder against the babies' parents and doctors. The charges were eventually dropped because a nurse was unable to absolutely link the parents and doctor to the order not to feed. The story had a happy and surprising ending. The boys were transferred to another Chicago hospital and eventually returned to their parents' care. Today, much to everyone's surprise, the twins have been separated, and are progressing well at home with their parents. Of course the boys need special care. Of course there are special problems in caring for the children. No, they probably will not be "normal." But the point is that the children are alive, progressing, and living independent lives.

The case of the Danville twins was a complicated medical situation. The boys had serious medical complications and for months doctors were not sure they could be separated. This is exactly the type of case pro-infanticide advocates point to as a "hopeless situation." Because the situation was medically complex and the complications were serious, they would advise death for the children. But the twins did not die and the case was far from hopeless.

Here again the initial decision not to treat was based on social and not medical factors. The decision not to provide oxygen and food to the twins was made before important medical information was available. There was no time to properly assess the boys' condition. The initial prognosis proved grossly inaccurate. No one can predict the medical future with certainty even in the most difficult cases. Someone's judgment that a situation is complex or complicated should never move us to kill the child.

Once again we must say that this cry of complexity is often no more than a smokescreen to hide the true motives of pro-infanticide advocates. They really want handicapped children removed from the scene, and they argue that situations are complex so that no one, especially advocates for the dying children, will examine such decisions. Many times, as in the case of Baby Doe, the case is much simpler than we are led to believe. But no situation is so complex that the principles of protecting life and providing care do not apply. No situation is so complex that starving the child becomes the best treatment option.

Words Make a Difference

Language plays an important role in the infanticide debate, just as it does in the struggle over abortion. Infanticide advocates often refer to starving a child as "letting nature take its course." The underlying idea seems to be that since the child would die anyway, we might as well help it along. Of course, *any* newborn child would die if merely left to the care of "nature." Each of us might die at some point in our lives if we just "let nature take its course." If you need an emergency appendectomy, you had better hope that authorities don't say, "Well, let's just let nature take its course."

Many times medical care is needed just so that nature will *not* take its course. But in the case of some handicapped newborn babies we want to refuse that medical treatment simply because the child is "imperfect." The phrase "letting nature take its course" masks the true intent of those who want to take a life because that life has no value to them.

Language helped cloud the issue in the case of Baby Doe. Supposedly Baby Doe's parents were convinced their child was "severely retarded" because he had Down's Syndrome and that he had no chance for any kind of meaningful future. In testimony taken from a brief to the U.S. Supreme Court, Dr. Walter Owens, Mrs. Doe's obstetrician, describes children with Down's Syndrome this way.

> I insisted upon telling the parents that this still would not be a normal child . . . that they did have another alternative which was to do nothing. In which case the child [would] probably live only a matter of several days . . . some of these children . . . are mere blobs.[2]

In fact, no child with Down's Syndrome is a "mere blob" and only a small percentage are severely retarded. In any case, no one can predict the level of retardation at birth. Baby Doe's parents had no way of assessing with certainty what kind of life their child would have had. We can be sure that it would have *not* been a life without hope or meaning. Many citizens with Down's Syndrome hold jobs, take the bus to work and live away from parents and family. Several persons with Down's Syndrome have even written books about their lives.

The recent case of Baby Jane Doe is another example of the way in which language clouds this issue. For weeks after her birth the media spoke of her as a severely retarded child who would be bedridden the remainder of her life. Her parents were portrayed as simply not wanting to prolong their child's suffering.

But in fact there was no conclusive evidence that Baby Jane suffered any retardation at all or that she would be bedridden. The truth is that Baby Jane was denied accepted medical treatment for a child in her condition. Baby Jane was denied the medical treatment that could have given her a meaningful life.

Another way of obscuring the issue is to emphasize the parents' heartbreak and their agonizing decision without reference to the rights of a helpless baby. Parents do face a difficult and emotionally stressful time when their child is born handicapped. But they are not the only ones who suffer. The child endures the death sentence. But media reports focus only upon the grief and agony of the parents. This redirects our attention from the true victim of nontreatment—the newborn baby.

Advocating a child's right to medically indicated treatment is not a complex request. It is simple and basic. It is something that no one would have questioned several years ago. We are asking for the right of every child, no matter now severely handicapped, to be treated exactly as a "normal" child would be. Handicapped children should be given the same medical treatment that would bring relief and healing. We are asking that a child not be denied treatment simply because he or she is handicapped.

How strange it is that we should have to fight so hard for

something that most of us take for granted—our protection as human beings under the law. Everyone is supposed to be equally protected under our legal system. Everyone is supposed to have access to care and treatment. Yet the rights of some handicapped newborns are ignored because someone thinks their lives are not worth living.

Let's look again at the case of Baby Jane Doe. In an editorial appearing in the *Chicago Tribune,* the writer advocated treatment for the baby girl. The piece was entitled "Baby Jane: Another View." Think about that title. The *alternative* viewpoint, the *minority opinion* in this case was to treat the child. What does it mean for us as a society when the minority opinion is to treat a baby? How far have we fallen into the quality of life world view when the majority of us think that denying a baby accepted medical treatment is the commonplace view?

FOUR

Treatment vs. Nontreatment

MEDICALLY SPEAKING infanticide boils down to one issue: to treat or not to treat the handicapped newborn. Remember that we are talking about a handicapped child who has a life-threatening condition that can be corrected and not a child who is born dying or who has no medical chance for survival.

Let's look at the pro-infanticide argument for nontreatment from the perspective of several doctors who adhere to this position. We will then critique that argument from the "prolife" perspective of another physician—Dr. C. Everett Koop, our nation's surgeon general.

The first question is why would a doctor decide not to treat a child who needed medical treatment?

An Unhappy Life?

Dr. Raymond S. Duff at Yale New Haven Hospital told fellow doctors in 1973 that he helped parents decide to kill their children because they were convinced this child had no "quality of life." They were convinced that their handicapped children would lead a life of suffering, agony, and unhappiness. In their view such a life was not worth living.

But can anyone really say that the handicapped person's life is unhappy? Dr. C. Everett Koop is one of our nation's finest pediatric surgeons. During his thirty-five years as a surgeon he pioneered many surgical advances to correct handicaps. In fact, he has probably operated on more babies with congenital defects than any surgeon in the country. His experience has taught him that the handicapped person's life is usually a full and happy life.

In 1977 Dr. Koop produced a film on infanticide with Francis Schaeffer.[1] In that film Dr. Koop asked eleven of his former patients to discuss their views on being handicapped before the cameras. The severity of the handicap varied with each individual. One patient has undergone thirty-seven operations to correct major defects at birth. Another was born without an esophagus, several children had tumors, cancer, or were missing other organs. None of these patients were coached on their answers.

These men and women were not leading miserable lives. One talked about "an added quality to my life—an appreciation of life." Another spoke of "life that is just worth living" and life that is "a gift—not something you can give, so you really don't have the right to take it either."

Many of these people would be candidates for infanticide if born today because doctors were convinced their lives would be miserable. Yet the truth is that they are capable, functioning human beings. Obviously, their road in life has been difficult. But, if anything, this difficulty has enhanced their appreciation of life.

In 1979, a British doctor who had specialized in treating patients with spina bifida wrote an anonymous article in *Lancet*. Early in his career he had treated children aggressively and had performed many lifesaving operations. He spoke of the courage and determination of his young patients, many of whom were now young adults, confined to a wheelchair and living with the effects of their handicap. The doctor admired these young people, but now he had changed his mind about treating them.

His patients' lives had convinced him that he should not treat babies born with spina bifida. He now advised parents to let their children starve to death. Obviously he had not asked his patients their views about their lives. He had simply concluded that because they did live with adversity, their lives were miserable. Because he was a doctor, he was in a position to impose these standards of happiness and unhappiness on others.

The doctor talked about what he would do if one of his patients came to him and asked him why he worked so hard to save his life.

> The question often occurs to me when talking to parents of a newborn baby with a severe handicap, what would I answer if the child when he came of age should ask me, "Why did you let me live?" My possible answers . . . sound hollow . . . The only answer which I could find . . . would be, "Your parents believed they could bring you up to be emotionally whole, though physically crippled."[2]

This doctor does not say that any of his *patients* had ever asked him that question. Nobody ever asked Dr. Koop that question either. In fact, he privately asked some parents if they were sorry he worked so hard to save their child's life. None of them had ever said yes.

Dr. Koop also asked fifty-three parents of children he had operated on what kind of impact the surgery had on their family. Only two responded that the effect was strong and negative. Seven said the effect was mild and negative. Ten said it was strong and positive and fourteen said it was mild and positive. Most interesting of all was the reaction of eighteen parents who said there was *no* impact at all.[3]

The person to ask about happiness and quality of life is the handicapped persons themselves. The evidence shows no connection between disability and unhappiness.

Cost Benefit Analysis

It has become common today to hear talk about the high cost of treating the handicapped child. We are often told how terribly expensive the treatment can be and we are told that medical resources are scarce. The costs are then compared with the benefits the patients receive from treatment. In other words, we are now being told we must make a cost benefit analysis of treating a handicapped child before we begin that treatment. After all, it is said, we do not want to waste valuable medical resources on a handicapped child when we could use that money to treat a "normal" infant.

The assumption of course is that the handicapped child is less of a person and therefore deserves less and not more of our medical attention. But how do you put a price tag on human life? How can we place more value on one life than on another.

Is it true that medical resources are scarce, so scarce that we must act now to make hard decisions about who lives and who dies? Many times this type of argument is used as a smoke-screen to mask the true intent of people who want to "weed out" the imperfect from society.

The United States is a very wealthy country. We funnel billions of dollars into the programs and priorities we think are important. Resources become "scarce" not so much because there are actual shortages as much as through priority decisions. Resources are *made* scarce. The fact is that human life has become cheap in our society and the life of a newborn handicapped infant is among the cheapest. We say we do not have the resources to treat handicapped newborns because we have not made them a priority.

Medical resources are not finite but are a function of the society's demand for medical resources. The issue is our view of life and the value we give to it. We have not come to the point in our society where we need to perform cost/benefit analyses on human lives because we are running out of money. The resources are there, but we have made decisions not to treat because we think of human life only in economic terms. We think the handicapped child is not a good investment.

Dr. Koop worked as a pediatric surgeon for many years. This is what he says about scarce medical resources:

> I can honestly say that, in thirty-five years I have been involved with the care of children, I have never felt that I was in a situation of finite medical resources. When I was short a bed, I could find one in an equivalent institution. When I was short of respirators, I could rent a spare. Whenever I needed extra hours of nursing support, I could always find an individual willing to go the extra mile.[4]

Dr. Koop found the medical resources he needed because he wanted to find them. Our society will also find those resources when it decides it wants to find them. It is also important to remember that any medical procedure is expensive when it is first tried. Costs come down when the treatment is perfected and used more commonly. Dr. Koop tells of an example at Children's Hospital in Philadelphia that illustrates this point. A newborn child was brought there with a severely infected bowel. There was very little hope for the baby, but she was placed on totally intravenous feeding while doctors waited for the possibility of a bowel transplant to give her a good chance of recovery. The baby died before a transplant was possible. She did, however, live on intravenous feedings for 400 days and she gained weight and developed well. This baby was the first ever to be placed on a totally intravenous feeding schedule. Doctors learned from her experience that this could be done. As Dr. Koop commented,

Although this little girl died, the experience gained with her, which was intentionally for her own good and not the good of society, did provide society with a new recognized technique that has saved the lives of millions of children and hundreds of thousands of adults throughout the world. In addition to that hospital stays have been shortened, wounds have healed more quickly and rehabilitation has been possible sooner (all with great savings in dollars).[5]

This baby girl was not used as an experiment. Doctors sought every aggressive treatment possible to relieve her condition. In her case the treatment was enormously expensive. But because doctors took the time and spent the money to try to save this baby's life, millions of future dollars were saved.

When we speaking of treating or not treating a handicapped baby, the only decisions to be made are medical decisions. Our own judgments about the child's quality of life, cost-benefit analyses and parental rights cannot be the basis for deciding who lives and dies. Every child, no matter how seriously handicapped, has a right to medical treatment. If anything, the seriously handicapped child has a right to more of our special care and attention.

FIVE

Parents' Rights

T HE IDEA THAT PARENTS should have the right to choose their child's death is the most powerful and persuasive argument that pro-infanticide forces have to offer. It is the argument we must dismantle if we are going to keep legalized infanticide from coming to America.

The parents' rights argument takes many different forms. One of the clearest examples of this viewpoint was expressed by Dr. Raymond Duff in 1973 in his famous article on the nontreatment of handicapped newborns. In Dr. Duff's words:

The burden of decision making must be borne by families . . . because they are most familiar with the respective situations. Since families primarily must live with . . . the decisions, it therefore appears that society and the health professions should provide only general guidelines for decision making. Moreover, since variations between situations are so great, and the situations themselves so complex, it follows that much latitude in decision making should be expected and tolerated.[1]

This argument is plausible on the surface, and many well-intentioned people have been taken in by it. In fact, doesn't the following argument sound all too familiar? "Parents traditionally have had authority over their children. Our courts have recognized these parental rights many times. Parents usually love their children and we assume that they will act in their children's best interests. Parents and families are also the people who bear the burdens of raising a handicapped child. They are the ones who must find the financial and emotional resources to deal with this new family member. In addition, each of these situations are extremely complex. There are many facets to be considered and only the family is able to analyse the many pieces of this 'tragic situation.' When we put all these factors together doesn't it make sense that parents should have the right to decide their child's fate? After all parents can decide the fate of their child before birth, why not give them the same power after birth. If the parents want their baby then every effort should be made to save the child. But if they don't want this child then we should 'let nature take its course.' Why not just carry the doctrine of 'every child a wanted child' one step further. If a *born* child is unwanted, let it die. (Or kill it.)"

Let's not think that only doctors and philosophers accept the parents' rights view on infanticide. A recent Phil Donahue show pertained to infanticide. His guest panel included a law professor who would not declare babies fully human until they had lived three months without abnormalities. Also present was a woman who had let her child die at birth, another woman who was raising her severely handicapped daughter, and a well-respected doctor who opposed infanticide.

The panel members argued the issue clearly, but much more interesting to me were the audience comments. Most of the women in the audience were probably basing their opinions on what they heard from the panelists. Over and over again they sympathized with infanticide. They thought the issue was too complex for anyone but the parents to decide. When the parents did make their agonizing decision, no one, including the law, should have the right to judge their conclusion. Very few women in the audience voiced the opinion that the child had any rights in this decision.

However appealing the parents' rights theory may be, it

cannot stand up to law or logic. American law has never recognized the absolute rights of parents over their children's lives. Even though we recognize a strong tradition of parental authority, we have also recognized the right of a child to live. Courts have ordered blood transfusions and surgery over the objections of parents when the life of the child is in danger. The newborn child is not a pawn in the hands of its parents. The child is an independent person with full protection under the law.

Secondly, the parents' rights theory subjects the life one person to the whim of another. It creates the same schizophrenia we now have with abortion. Any pregnant woman in this country can find out that she is carrying a handicapped child and then legally destroy that child before birth. Suppose two pregnant women discover they are both carrying a child with Down's Syndrome. One woman wants her child to live; the other woman aborts her child. Both children had every chance for a happy, hopeful life. But only one of them has the opportunity to live that life. The parents' rights theory says that what can happen three months before birth can happen three days after birth. Children will be killed, not because they are dying, but because parents won't give them the right to live. One family would decide to let their handicapped baby live because he was "wanted," yet another child, with exactly the same handicap, would die because his parents did not want him.

We need to ask ourselves whether all parents always act in the best interests of their children? Do all parents love their children so much that they are willing to sacrifice their dream of a "normal" child to raise a handicapped child? We live in a society where we destroy unborn children because they are the wrong sex. What makes us think that we can tolerate 1.6 million abortions a year and still have a society where parents unconditionally accept their newborn children? How can we think that the mentality of easy abortion and cheap life will not infect our attitudes toward our newborn children?

We must realize that parent's feelings for their children are very subjective and often have nothing to do with their child's medical state. Phillip Becker, a teenager with Down's Syndrome who needed a lifesaving operation, is an example. Phillip's natural parents refused the operation. After a long controversy and a court battle, Phillip was adopted and his new parents authorized the surgery.

Phillip's natural and adoptive parents differed completely in their opinion of him. Phillip's real father thought "it would be best for everyone" if his son died quickly. The Heaths, Phillip's adoptive parents, looked forward to a long life with their new son. The Beckers visited their son only several times a year in the institution where they had placed him. A California court said the bond between the Heaths and Phillip was so strong that they had become his "psychological parents." They had taken Phillip home with them often and spent long hours with him at the state home. They saw him as a happy, loving teenager who was now a welcome member of their family.

Phillip is the same child for both sets of parents. It was the parental *attitudes* that would make one think the Beckers and his adopted parents were describing two different boys. As it is in Phillip's case, so it is with so many other handicapped children. It is the parent's attitude toward their child that can make the difference. It is often on the basis of these attitudes that children are denied necessary treatment. Surely, we cannot hand a child's life over to their parents when we know that parents' value judgments may be completely opposed to their child's best interests.

Dr. Duff gives an example of what can happen in his article about withholding treatment at Yale-New Haven Hospital:

An infant with Down's Syndrome and intestinal atresia, like the much publicized one at Johns Hopkins Hospital, was not treated because his parents thought that surgery was wrong for their baby and themselves. He died several days after birth.[2]

Let's translate this paragraph. The baby died of starvation several days later because his parents refused to give their consent for a routine operation that would have allowed him to take nourishment and live. Why did these parents think surgery was wrong for their baby? The obvious answer is because their child was handicapped.

What does parents' rights mean when it comes to infanticide? It means that we hand the child's right to life over to the parents. Whatever protection the law might give to persons is denied the handicapped newborn solely because he is handicapped. The newborn child, just like the unborn child, becomes an extension of its parents. If those parents do not want their child then they have the right to kill their baby.

Most parents who are reading this will probably find it hard to understand how some parents have a hard time deciding whether their baby should live. My husband and I have some personal experience with a life-threatening situation involving our son, Will.

Like many Down's Syndrome children, Will required an early operation. In this case a blockage developed in his stomach when he was five weeks old and immediate surgery was required. Never did it occur to us or to any of our doctors to even think about not performing the surgery because Will had Down's Syndrome. There was no hesitation on anyone's part. The only choices to make were where and when to perform the surgery. There was nothing difficult about our decision. Our baby needed help and like most parents, we wanted to do everything to be sure he got the best possible care.

But this is no longer the universal reaction. Parents talk about the agonizing decision they faced when they decided to kill their child with a drug overdose. They refuse surgery. They bring death to a baby who has every chance for life.

It is true that in many of these cases, the parents and doctors are uninformed. Parents mistakenly take the advice of ignorant doctors, believing that there is no hope for their baby. They honestly believe that they are simply saving their child from a painful and slow death.

But there is another attitude at work that needs to be brought out in the open. We are witnessing a breakdown in the bond of parental love. Somehow we have accepted the idea that we have a right to a perfect child. After all when we plan and prepare so carefully for a baby, we think that the baby should measure up to our standards. When our child is imperfect, we do not want him. We do not want to make the extra sacrifices, take the extra time, and deal with the extra emotional and physical stress that this child can bring.

Parents have always sacrificed for their children. The bond between parent and child is probably the strongest in the world. Most parents would die for their children. Yet now we are witnessing a new kind of parent. It is the parent who has a child for the personal satisfaction that the child can bring them. That child must measure up to a certain set of standards or forfeit its life. This parent is willing to make some limited sacrifices for their child as long as they do not involve too much emotional and physical energy on the parents' part.

What we are witnessing here is a breakdown in the basic "glue" of society. What we are seeing is parents without an unconditional love for their children. Mother Teresa once asked, "If a mother can kill her child, what can be next?" Indeed, what can be next if we lose this most basic bond between parent and child. What makes the decision to kill your child so difficult? For some parents the difficulty must be in deciding whether your child's life or your own lifestyle will come first.

SIX

The Law and Infanticide

INFANTICIDE, LIKE ABORTION is very much a legal issue. Legally, abortion on demand came to us in one decision, on one day. Legalized infanticide could come in exactly the same way. What happens in our nation's courts will determine the fate of handicapped newborn babies in this country.

The most important point to remember about the law and infanticide is this: *the law protects the handicapped newborn infant exactly the same way as it protects a full-grown healthy adult citizen.* The newborn child, no matter how retarded or impaired, has exactly the same rights under the Constitution as you and I do. The newborn person is a legal person protected by our laws. No amount of talk about the parents' rights or "meaningful life" can change this fact.

Furthermore, parents, doctors, and hospitals have a legal responsibility to treat all handicapped newborns and the law holds them accountable when they fail to do so. Law Professor John Robertson has listed the crimes that doctors and parents may commit when they refuse to treat handicapped infants:

—Every state imposes a duty upon parents to care for their children. When they fail to uphold this duty and their child dies they can be prosecuted for manslaughter or murder. Care for a child cannot be withheld because of cost, or parents' wishes.

—Parents can also be prosecuted under child abuse laws for

failure to care for their children, and for cruelty or neglect in failing to provide necessary medical care.

—The doctor and hospital have a contractual obligation to provide treatment when they admit a patient or enter a case. This obligation remains in force even if parents do not give their consent to treatment for their child.

—If parents refuse treatment the doctor and hospital may ask the parents to remove the child from their care or they may ask a court to appoint a guardian who can consent to treatment on behalf of the child.

—The doctor who counsels the parents to withold treatment or who merely agrees with their decision can be guilty of failure to report child abuse in at least twenty states.

—Since reporting the abuse of the child might have saved the child's life, the doctor who fails to report nontreatment could be guilty of manslaughter.

—The doctor may be guilty of murder by omission because he did not uphold his duty to care for the child and as a result of his nontreatment, the child died.

—The doctor has a legal duty to care for the child and to report when the child under his care is being neglected. The doctor could withdraw his treatment or decide not to treat the child only if he has notified public authorities who would act to protect the child.

—The doctor has also a legal duty to protect the child. By his providing information to the parents the child may be imperiled.

—The doctor may also be subject to prosecution for murder because he is an accessory to the death of the child. A doctor who counseled or encouraged parents not to treat their child would be someone who "counsels, encourages, or aids . . . another to commit a felony."[1]

—Nurses who withhold treatment are also at risk. In some cases a nurse is responsible to act in opposition to doctor's orders if protection of the patient requires it. In another case the courts have found that nurses have a duty to at least report such a situation to their supervisor.

—Doctors could also raise a petition to a court to treat a child over the parents' objections. In such a case the court is likely to grant treatment as it did in the 1974 *Houle* case in Maine. In this case, parents refused consent for surgery to correct a badly formed esophagus in their newborn child. The baby had an unknown measure of brain damage and no left eye or ear. In this case the court showed itself to be a strong protector of newborn life:

> At the moment of birth there does exist a human being entitled to the fullest protection of the law. The most basic right enjoyed by every human being is the right to life itself. The issue before the court is not the quality of life to be preserved. Being satisfied that corrective surgery is medically necessary and medically feasible, the court finds that the defendants have no right to withhold such treatment.[2]

Similarly, in New York in 1979 the court appointed a guardian for a baby girl with spina bifida in order that surgery could be performed to close the lesion on her back. The parents had wanted to take their baby girl home to "let God decide" if she should live. The court overruled them and ordered treatment for the child so that she could live and reach her fullest potential.

It is clear that the law stands on the side of the handicapped newborn. But if our Constitution so clearly protects handicapped children, then why have we not seen more cases of infanticide brought to trial? This lack of prosecutions shows just how close pro-infanticide forces are to winning the battle for legalized infanticide. The laws are on the books, but they are ignored or neglected by those who would choose death as a treatment option.

There are several reasons why the law seems to look the

other way in the issue of infanticide. Infanticide is a difficult and emotional issue; no one likes to handle it. Nurses, who are so often caught in the middle, are afraid to testify against doctors or parents. For example, parents and a doctor were indicted for neglect of the Siamese twins in Danville, Illinois, but at a preliminary hearing a nurse could not remember if the parents were truly linked with the order not to feed the twins. From a doctor's perspective it takes great courage to testify against fellow colleagues and risk professional ouster.

Another reason why infanticide does not get into court is the widespread belief that parents should be able to let handicapped children die if they wish. Sympathy often lies with parents, and prosecutors are not likely to bring them to court.

Wrongful Life and Wrongful Birth

The law uncompromisingly protects the handicapped newborn baby; infanticide is illegal. On the other hand, a new trend is developing in the law that has frightening implications for unborn and newborn human life. This is a new legal theory known as "wrongful life." That it should be taken seriously shows how far the sanctity of life worldview has been eroded in our society.

In a "wrongful life" case, a handicapped child sues the doctors and perhaps his own parents for having allowed him to be born. The theory behind "wrongful life" suits is that life with a handicap is worse than no life at all. These children are saying that it would have been better not to have been born.

Until recently courts rejected this kind of logic. For example, in a 1967 New Jersey case, the court refused to award damages to a child who was born with Down's Syndrome. In its decision the court noted that one of the

> most deeply held beliefs in our society is that life—whether experienced with or without a major handicap—is more

precious than non-life . . . To rule otherwise would require us to disavow the basic assumption upon which our society is based . . . (and) [t]his we cannot do.[3]

The court recognized that human life was a sacred value to be preserved and that no court could take it upon itself to make "quality of life" decisions about who would be better off not having been born.

In 1980, however, the California Court of Appeals took a different position. The court recognized the claim of a girl born with Tay-Sachs disease. The court noted that the Supreme Court's *Roe* v. *Wade* decision legalizing abortion made it legal for a woman to abort her handicapped child. In light of that decision the court raised the idea that a child could sue its parents if the parents chose to let it live with a handicap instead of having it aborted.

The court argued that "if a case arose where, despite due care by the medical profession in transmitting the necessary warnings, the parents made a conscious choice to proceed with a pregnancy, with full knowledge that a seriously impaired infant would be born . . . we see no sound public policy that should protect those parents from being answerable for the pain, suffering and misery that they have wrought upon their offspring."[4] In other words, parents have a legal duty *not* to let their child be born if the child is handicapped because life with a handicap is worse than no life at all.

Fortunately in 1982, the California Supreme Court diluted this reasoning and found only a limited theory of wrongful life.

But even if courts have basically rejected wrongful life cases they have easily accepted wrongful birth cases. These are cases where the parents of a handicapped child sue the doctor for not giving them information about birth defects that would have led them to abort the baby. At least nine states have recognized the validity this type of case. They claim that doctors should be held accountable for their negligence in not informing parents about possible handicaps.

But the real theory behind such cases is that it was is wrong for some human beings to have been born. In a wrongful birth case, parents say that they would have killed their child if they had all the facts. They are suing the doctor because he did not give them the facts. In other words, life with a handicap is worse than no life at all. "Wrongful life" or "wrongful birth" mean that it was "wrong" for this life to be born. The phrases imply that society is wrong to give its protection to such life.

The acceptance of wrongful birth suits creates a climate that encourages the elimination of handicapped children, both unborn and newborn. As such suits become more common, a doctor, fearing that he will be sued, will be careful to advise parents to have tests done for genetic defects and he will tell them about the availability of abortion. This type of testing is already well on the way to becoming standard medical practice. It will allow parents to abort handicapped children before birth. It also leads to infanticide. Doctors may be more likely to advise parents not to treat a handicapped newborn if he suspects that the parents may one day sue him for a "wrongful birth" action.

Wrongful life suits threaten the protection handicapped children receive under the state's criminal laws. If we do not challenge the theory of these suits—that it is wrong for some lives to be lived—we may eventually decide not to protect these lives.

Pro-infanticide forces are working hard to change the laws so that the laws protect the parents and not the child. They want to hand the child's right to life over to the parents and make that baby's life dependent upon the good-will of the parents. We need to resist these efforts, including those theories in the law which tell us that some lives are not worth living.

The Equal Treatment Standard

If parents' wishes and "social" factors shouldn't determine the fate of a handicapped baby, what standards should we use?

How can we decide when treatment will only prolong the dying process and when it is vital to the health and future of the child.

The proper standard is known in the law as "equal protection." Simply put, it means that if a treatment would be given to a "normal" child, the same treatment should be given to a handicapped child. Parents' wishes and quality of life factors do not enter into the decision. It's as simple as that.

Infanticide is a civil rights issue, a newly-noticed aspect of the struggle for equal rights. When a newborn baby is denied necessary treatment simply because he or she is handicapped, the baby suffers discrimination. A baby, just like a fully grown adult, is fully protected under our laws. Surely death by starvation is the ultimate form of discrimination. How ironic it is that at the same time we work so hard to provide equal access to public buildings for our physically disabled citizens, we deny the most basic medical treatment to our youngest and most helpless citizens.

This "equal protection" framework can help us deal with many situations that look difficult. If a child is born dying due to a handicap, certain treatments are not required, just as they are not always required with non-handicapped patients who are terminally ill. But in the case of a child born with Down's Syndrome or spina bifida, surgery to repair a badly deformed esophagus would be required if a "normal" child would have the surgery.

The federal government applied this standard in its "Baby Doe" regulations issued in 1983. The rules required hospitals to place a notice stating that "Discriminatory failure to feed or care for handicapped infants in this facility is prohibited by federal law." The government's strategy was to attack infanticide by simply pointing out that discrimination against handicapped people is prohibited by federal law. Hospitals can lose their federal funding if they practice this form of discrimination. The rules made it clear that no hospital was required to administer "futile therapies" or therapies that would only prolong a child's dying.

The notices hospitals were required to post really did not say anything new. They were a restatement, merely a reminder to the hospitals about a law that had been on the books for the last ten years.

The "Baby Doe" rule was a bold step forward in the protection of handicapped newborns. But from the day the rules were announced they have created a storm of controversy, a controversy that continues. Oddly enough, doctors to whom we entrust the care of our children have been at the center of the storm.

Immediately after the rules were issued, the American Academy of Pediatrics (the "AAP"), representing 25,000 pediatricians in the U.S., filed suit to prevent the rules from going into effect. The pediatricians claimed that the rules were an intrusion into the doctor/patient relationship and interfered with treatment decisions that are so complex that only doctors can understand them.

Judge Gerhard Gesell of the U.S. District Court in Washington, D.C., ruled in favor of the pediatricians. Steven Baer, writing in the *National Review*, commented that "the real problem is this: Judge Gesell . . . seems to doubt that handicapped children are people."[5]

In knocking down the Baby Doe regulations, Judge Gesell stated that some handicapped infants may indeed be persons and entitled to the protection of the law. But he refused to say just what other handicapped infants—those who did not fit the definition of person—might be called. In other words, Judge Gesell left the door to legalized infanticide wide open. He did so by declining to plainly state that all handicapped infants should be protected under the law.

The Reagan administration persisted. It issued new rules after a sixty-day period during which the public was invited to comment. Over ninety-six percent of those written comments favored the regulations. It was also during this time that *Pediatrics* journal published the infamous commentary comparing severely handicapped infants to dogs and pigs.

After the Reagan administration issued the revised rules, the AAP and other health groups sat down to work out a compromise on the regulations. After months of negotiation, the government retained the rules and the hotline number, but also encouraged hospitals to set up ethical review boards to review specific cases of non-treatment at the hospitals.

In the case of abortion, ethical review boards paved the way for more liberal abortion laws. But this does not have to be the case with infanticide. It is true that there are really no ethics to review in these cases. Either the child should receive medical treatment or the case is medically hopeless. However, the AAP protested the Baby Doe rules so strenuously that the administration was forced to concede the ethics committee approach to them.

The point to remember is that now we must *work* to be sure that those who honor the sanctity of life of every person are members of these committees. We can be sure that those who want to base treatment decisions on factors like the baby's quality of life will find places on these committees. Our responsibility is to be certain that we make our voices heard.

What does this controversy about the Baby Doe regulations tell us? For one thing, it tells us how far the medical profession has strayed from the role of healer.

The Baby Doe Rules were simple regulations requiring that hospitals not discriminate against handicapped newborns. They did not interfere with a doctor's exercise of his best medical judgment. The rules were entirely consistent with the age-old tradition that physicians heal and care for the sick, especially the most needy and helpless. Certainly handicapped newborns fall into this category.

Yet the American Academy of Pediatrics and other organizations representing health care professionals denounced the rule. Their claim that the rule interferes with the doctor/patient relationship flies in the face of the facts. It was only when doctors strayed beyond medical judgments that the regulations would be applied. Why would the medical profession take such a strong stand against this rule? The plainest answer is that many in the AAP and other medical groups do not want to be healers to the handicapped newborn. Perhaps many of them favor death as the best option they can offer to these newborn babies.

The "Baby Doe" rules are also an example of what can happen when the courts get hold of an issue like infanticide. Judge Gesell made his views plain when he sided with the AAP. Although the anti-discrimination law on which the Baby Doe rules were based applied to all persons, he questioned whether the laws about discrimination should apply specifically to infants.

Judge Gesell's decision is a clear example of pro-infanticide thinking in the courts. Although this was just one case, Judge Gesell's opinions could be used by future courts to help pave the way for legalized infanticide. His opinions were the views of just one man. In this case, however, one man's opinion could help change the law of the land. This controversy over the Baby Doe regulations is just one more example of the important role the courts play in the human life issues.

We must continue to stress the equal protection standard when we discuss these issues. The handicapped child, no matter how severely affected, is entitled to the same protection as any other infant or adult. The idea that all human life has equal value is the cornerstone of our legal system. To deny this protection to a handicapped baby is to take away the sole defense of one of our most helpless citizens.

SEVEN

Attitudes Toward the Handicapped

C HANGING ATTITUDES TOWARD the handicapped are working hand in hand with the devaluation of human life which makes infanticide possible. Most of us never enter the world of the handicapped persons. Ninety-six percent of children in this country are born "normal." Handicapped people are "different." We all have a natural aversion to someone we don't understand, to someone who does not or cannot act in the same way we act.

Some think that death might be the best option for some handicapped children because they think real people are "normal" people. They also think that being different means being less. Both of these attitudes are common in our society and both of them are worth examining to help us understand this issue.

We are a nation accustomed to perfection. Our application of technology coupled with ever-growing affluence has given us "the best of everything." Everything should always work. When it doesn't work we throw it away. When we want something, we expect to get it now.

The expectation of having everything we want and having it work perfectly spills over into our attitudes toward children. Children are no longer viewed as an indispensable and totally natural part of life. We no longer ask a young couple "When are you going to have children?" but "*Are* you going to have children?" For many people, having children has to be balanced against the new condominium in the mountains or the second car they won't be able to have if they have a baby. Children for many have become ornaments that they choose to add to their lives.

I have seen this attitude in several close friends. These talented young women are rising to top spots in their careers. Unmarried, they have always had time to devote to travel and the long hours necessary to be successful in their professions. Yet now, in their early thirties they find themselves with a strong desire to have a baby. These women talk often about the experience of having a baby. It's clear that the feeling of giving birth and being a mother is more important than a husband, family, or even the actual baby. In other words, parenthood for them is a very self-centered experience. They want to have a child before it's too late because they don't want to miss out on something. They have had the best of everything until now and a child will complete their dream of the perfect life.

Naturally, these women expect their child to be "normal." In a plan so carefully prepared and calculated, a handicapped child is not welcome. These women are achievement-oriented professionals and they would expect the same from their children. If the child isn't normal then abortion, or even infanticide, could become the chosen "treatment option."

Of course not every young professional couple or single career woman has imbibed these attitudes of liberal motherhood. Happily, the bonds of parental love and maternal affection are often stronger than these ideas. Mothers can sacrifice for their children in spite of what they have been taught. But the idea of perfection runs deep in the present generation and it contributes to a cultural climate that condones infanticide.

Several years ago I met a young couple at a gathering of lawyers. Both were attorneys and the woman was five months pregnant. As we talked she told me that she had recently had an amniocentesis test and was waiting to see if her child was "normal." I asked what she would do if the test revealed her baby had a handicap. Her quick answer was abortion. In fact she had had an abortion the previous year because their careers had made having a child inconvenient.

This woman told me that she and her husband just did not have room in their lives for a handicapped child. What would have happened if their test had failed and the baby was born with a handicap? No one can say what they would have chosen. But we do know that the odds were stacked against that child from the beginning. Choosing life in this case would have been difficult at best.

We want what we want when we want it and we want it to be perfect. In that world view a child with a handicap just doesn't have a chance.

Why is it that perfection is often our only standard? Many times it is because we believe that being different means being less. A "normal" child and a "normal" adult do certain things. Those who cannot do these things are less of a human being.

I read about a couple who had decided to keep their baby boy with Down's Syndrome. They considered an abortion when they learned several months before birth that their child carried the Down's trait. But they had decided that their love and home was the best place for their child.

In the course of their decision-making they consulted with the director of a home for handicapped citizens. The parents kept telling the director about the things their child would never be able to do. He would never go to the prom, or play high school football, or go to college. To every comment like this the director's answer was the same: "But many normal children never do that." Finally the child's mother understood. "But what is normal?" she asked.

That is exactly the point. "Normal" is a very relative and subjective term. Indeed, it can be a meaningless term. Every person varies according to potential and capabilities. Just because a person cannot do some task does not mean he is less of a human being. Capabilities vary from person to person but humanity is there in full from the beginning. We often judge individuals in terms of their abilities and then set a standard for what every "normal" person should be. Instead, we should be looking at each person as a unique human being with a unique potential to fulfill. Our task is to help that person fulfill their potential, whatever it might be.

A friend told me about a visit he had with a family in Indiana. My friend has been active in the pro-life movement and had gone to Indiana to fulfill a speaking engagement. A woman had invited him to her home because she thought a visit with their two year old daughter might encourage my friend in his work.

At the home of this farm family he found a beautiful two-year-old girl dressed in a blue sailor suit sleeping in her crib. But this child was really quite different. She was born with major portions of her brain missing. In fact, if you held her head close to a light you could almost see through to the back of her head. Doctors diagnosed her as a "hopeless case," but this farm family had adopted the baby girl and showered their love and faith upon her.

The girl had made great progress. At two years of age she was able to communicate her needs through different sounds, listen responsively to different kinds of music and gaze intently into her mother's eyes, even though she has no optic nerve. Doctors are convinced that she does, in some sense, see. They had predicted she would never be able to move and yet now she can lift up her head. The strides this child has made are nothing short of miraculous. Much of the credit must go to the love of her parents.

But as this mother talked with my friend it was obvious that her child's accomplishments were secondary to her. She had brought my friend to see the full humanity of this little girl. By most standards her accomplishments were minimal. She would never be a "normal child." But as her mother commented, "Her soul is completely whole." When this woman looked at her child she saw a complete human being. Although her physical and mental capacities were limited, her character, her essential personhood were fully present.

Many times we practice a subtle yet powerful form of discrimination against our handicapped citizens by believing that being different means being less. I saw this kind of attitude illustrated in a discussion with college students about a hypothetical "life boat" situation they had been discussing in an ethics class. Twelve people were on a lifeboat and only seven could be saved. It was important to pick the right seven because a nuclear holocaust had destroyed the world and the seven survivors would have to create a new civilization. The candidates included among others, a priest, a social worker, a mathematician and a handicapped person.

For many the handicapped person was the first to be sacrificed. After all, only the strongest, the fittest, the "best" were needed in the new world. The handicapped survivor would be a burden. In their eyes he was "of less value" than the other survivors. But several students chose the handicapped man first to remain in the lifeboat. It was difficult for them to put their reasons into words, but they were convinced that this person had something important and uniquely his own to contribute to the new society. In their opinion being different did not mean being less.

Often we think we have so much to offer our handicapped citizens. But many times it is they who have so much to offer us. They can show us the courage, determination and perseverance that they have developed from painstakingly learning so many tasks we take for granted. Hasn't each of us seen moral courage illustrated by a blind man "seeing" his way along a sidewalk with a white cane? Handicapped people demonstrate to us the simplicity, joy, and love of a life that has been stripped of the striving for status and prestige that consumes so many of us.

A pastor friend of ours lost his oldest daughter to a brain tumor. A week after her death he returned to his congregation to preach the Sunday morning service. After the service many parishoners found it difficult to talk to their pastor. But one young handicapped man did understand that the pastor had lost someone he loved very much. This young man, who has very limited language skills, came up, put his arm around the pastor, and pointed to his own shoulder. He was letting the pastor know that he cared and if he wanted to put his head on his shoulder and have a good cry, it was fine with him. That young man, in his simple and loving way, expressed the thoughts of so many in that congregation that day.

Our attitudes about handicapped citizens will play a crucial role in keeping legalized infanticide from coming to America. If we accept the idea that handicapped lives are not worth living, nothing will stop infanticide. But if we uphold our ideas of the dignity and worth of every human life and publicly state our views, we can stop this injustice. Perhaps we all need to rethink our ideas about what it means to be a person and make a contribution in society.

EIGHT

Down's Syndrome

DOWN'S SYNDROME, and spina bifida are two of society's most common handicaps. Several of the cases we have discussed in this chapter involved children with these conditions. Yet, even though these handicaps are common, most of us know very little about either condition. Indeed it has only been within the last twenty years that researchers and doctors have begun to understand the causes and treatment of these handicaps. The facts about Down's Syndrome and spina bifida are surprising and they give us a hopeful picture for the future. Our knowledge about these handicaps can help family and friends of handicapped children better understand and cope with their child's condition.

Down's syndrome, named after Dr. Langdon Down, is the most common handicap in our society. It has been with us for centuries and is known to occur in roughly one out of seven hundred families.

Until recently infants with Down's Syndrome were put in institutions from birth. Frequently, parents never saw their children. Ignorant doctors told them that their child was an "idiot" and would never live past the teenage years. The child was labelled a "mongoloid" because of often apparent "oriental" features such as slightly slanted eyes and a flatness in facial features. It was assumed that the child's life was hopeless.

In the last several decades Down's Syndrome has become the subject of intense study. It was only in the 1950s that technological advances helped identify the extra chromosome that is responsible for the physical and mental characteristics of Down's Syndrome.

It was also during these years that parents, doctors, and educators began to realize the abilities and potentials of the person with Down's Syndrome. Far from being severely retarded, the majority of children with Down's Syndrome are mildly or moderately retarded. When taken out of the sterile environment of a state home, the children showed dramatic improvements in physical and mental abilities. They responded well to all types of stimulation and exhibited an almost extraordinary ability to give and receive love. When placed in a loving and stimulating environment at home and school the child with Down's Syndrome developed skills that enabled him to take a job in the community or a sheltered workshop. Many adults with the Down's trait are now living away from home, in supervised apartments with other handicapped adults. Some citizens with Down's Syndrome have even written books and married.[1]

We have come to realize that the citizen with Down's Syndrome is first and foremost a human being who can experience love, hope and fulfillment like anyone else. They are capable of loving and learning and functioning in society just like every citizen in our country.

Dr. Jerome LeJeune, a French physician, first identified the extra chromosome that causes Down's Syndrome. The child with Down's Syndrome has forty-seven instead of forty-six chromosomes in each cell of his body. Each of us receives twenty-three chromosomes from our father and mother. The Down's Syndrome child receives an extra #21 chromosome from one parent. There are several forms of Down's Syndrome, but the most common form is known as Trisomy 21. Parents of children with Trisomy 21 have a 1-2 percent chance of having another baby with Down's Syndrome.

This extra chromosome accounts for a variety of mental and physical characteristics. The baby with Down's Syndrome can often be identified by facial features such as slanted eyes or a short, stubby nose, or by a distinctive crease across the palm. Although visual identification is usually possible at birth it is sometimes necessary to do a chromosome analysis to make a diagnosis.

Thirty to forty percent of children with Down's Syndrome have heart defects of some kind. Some have faulty digestive systems. Most of these defects are correctable with prompt treatment or surgery. Only a very small percentage of these problems are incompatible with life.

Although a diagnosis of Down's Syndrome may be confirmed at birth it is impossible to predict the degree of retardation the child will have. We now realize that the child with Down's Syndrome is his or her own unique person—just like any other child. There is as much diversity and variation between these children as with any other group of children. The stereotype of a short, fat, severely retarded person with tongue hanging out and unable to speak is grossly inaccurate.

While the child with Down's Syndrome does learn, grow, and achieve like any other child, he does so at a slower pace. The baby with Down's Syndrome will lift his head, roll over, sit up, crawl, and walk like any other child. But he will do so at a later age.

An ordinary child may walk at twelve months but the child with Down's Syndrome may walk at nineteen to twenty-nine months. He will learn to feed himself, be toilet trained and dress himself too, but it may take him longer to learn than other children.

The keys to helping any baby or child with Down's Syndrome are stimulation and early intervention. A child with Down's Syndrome needs more stimulation and encouragement to respond to his environment. The extra stimulation that comes with attractive toys, music, colorful clothing and different textures are particularly important to the baby with

Down's Syndrome. Because they often have low muscle tone, the child with Down's Syndrome may be less active than other children. It is not enough to put an attractive toy in front of them. They may need extra help to reach the toy and learn how it works. The important thing to remember is that they will learn. With extra help and encouragement they will explore their world.

I know some of these things about Down's Syndrome from personal experience with our own little boy, Will. Will had the low muscle tone at birth characteristic of children with Down's Syndrome. In a resting position he was very limp and relaxed. While he was still an infant, we began a program of stimulation and exercise. A therapist showed us different exercises to encourage lifting the head and rolling over. We tickled him often, sang to him, placed colorful and musical toys within his reach. We introduced him to as many friends as possible.

This stimulation seemed to get results. At three months Will rolled over, and at seven months he sat alone and made his first moves toward crawling. He was far from being an inactive baby. At six months he rolled everywhere, explored all his toys, and generally kept me busy twenty-four hours a day.

Of course we know that a slowdown is coming. Just because Will is progressing at a "normal" pace now does not mean he will walk at a year or that his growth will continue at this pace. It does mean that our Will is off to the best possible start and that he is already beginning to build the skills he will need for the future. It's never too early to begin to stimulate and encourage the baby with Down's Syndrome. Parents, family and friends have a very important part to play in helping their child. No matter how slow the progress may seem at times, that baby will develop.

Education is vital for the child with Down's Syndrome. It is the key to the child's success in fulfilling his or her unique potential. It is true that an adult with Down's Syndrome may never go to college (although several have attended college).

But they can become contributing members of society through education.

Down's Syndrome children often need "special" education. "Special" means taking extra time to learn the skills needed to teach the retarded child. Often the child with Down's Syndrome needs the different parts of a learning task explained, demonstrated, or broken down into simpler parts. Nothing can be taken for granted and often learning is much slower. It takes patience, creativity, and understanding to give this special kind of education.

Nursery school is often the first school experience for a child with the Down's trait. At three years they learn "people skills," community interaction and independence. The school can be a "normal" nursery school or a special school or better yet a "special" classroom set within a public school. The important thing is that the child receives an enriching experience that encourages him to learn more and expand his abilities when he enters school.

Many people often wonder if school is necessary or "worth it" for the Down's Syndrome child. School is as important to him as it is for any child. School gives a child a chance to learn self-respect and confidence. The child learns that he is capable of achieving and interacting with others in the community. He learns the skills that will help him take his place in the community. It is no different for children with Down's Syndrome. Academically they are limited, although they can and should be taught to read, write and do arithmetic. But school provides them with the many skills they need for the future. Arts and crafts, music, speech and language all contribute to the overall education of every child, and especially the child with Down's Syndrome. Extra activities like Brownies, Cub Scouts, and Girl Scouts provide the group interaction and enrichment every child needs.

Many times Down's Syndrome children are unnecessarily separated from "normal" children in school. This may sometimes be necessary, but it is often harmful to the child and the class. The child with Down's Syndrome needs to be "main-streamed" with other children as much as possible. It is assumed frequently that because the child has Down's Syndrome he cannot function in the classroom. Often the child's unique abilities are overlooked simply because the child is labelled a "Down's Syndrome child." The child with Down's Syndrome will ordinarily respond to the stimulation of the normal classroom and achieve much more than he or she otherwise would if separated from other children.

It is also true that "normal" children have much to learn from the child with Down's Syndrome. Soon after Will was born I visited a "special education" class of preschoolers. The classroom of eight preschoolers was set within a regular public school and staffed by a specially trained teacher and a full-time aide. It was amazing to watch these children progress in social and behavioral skills.

But even more amazing was the way in which all of these children had been adopted by the other gradeschoolers. As they walked from class to recess, older children waved, called out hello, and even left their games just to come say "Hi." Fifth and sixth graders helped the teacher with the children during recess and volunteered as helpers during special projects.

One touching incident illustrated the warm relationship between the children. Earlier in the year the special preschool class had participated, along with every other class, in the school Christmas pageant. They had worked for months to practice a simple song and dance. But when the moment came to go "on stage" they panicked. The children forgot their songs and froze on stage. But suddenly and spontaneously the children in the audience began to applaud and gave the children a standing ovation. It was a wonderful show of support and it was just the encouragement the children needed to finish their number in their own special way.

Those children, in so many ways, had made an impact on children and teachers at that school. Positive attitudes and values toward the handicapped citizen were being formed at an early age because someone had made the commitment to bring a "special" class to that school. Of course, the preschoolers were benefiting from all the stimulation of a public school. But just as important, the other children were learning that being different doesn't mean being less. In so many ways those children needed each other.

The citizen with Down's Syndrome needs a place to participate in the community. Education means an education for a lifetime. It includes pre-vocational training to help young people decide what tasks might interest them. Although the horizons for a retarded person may seem limited to us, the opportunities are many. Depending on their individual abilities, the young adult with Down's Syndrome can work in the community or in a sheltered workshop setting. In our town, a young man with Down's Syndrome works at the supermarket as a bag boy. He is neat, efficient, friendly, and does his job well. A combination work-study program in school can help build and develop the skills and good work habits that will lead to job success.

The goal of work is the same for a person with Down's Syndrome as it is with any other adult. Work brings satisfaction, builds confidence, and contributes to the community. Given the opportunity and encouragement, the person with Down's Syndrome can and does make that contribution.

For many years the parents of Down's Syndrome children believed their child would always be living with them. A more independent life away from home seemed like an impossibility. Yet today, many mentally handicapped adults are living away from parents and family in supervised group apartment residences. When we consulted with the geneticist to discuss our own son's future she told us that we should expect Will to live away from home and that we should begin to help him set those goals for himself during his teenage years. Just as we would discuss college with other children, we should also discuss Will's future with him and help him direct his life toward those goals.

Our handicapped citizens have a valuable contribution to make to our society; the person with Down's Syndrome is no exception. They may need more of our help and attention. The rewards are worth the extra effort. Love, education and training will enable the citizen with Down's Syndrome to fulfill the unique potential God has given them.

NINE

Spina Bifida

FOR EVERY THOUSAND CHILDREN born in the U.S., between one and two have spina bifida. Thus it is one of the most common handicaps. Spina bifida occurs when a baby's spinal cord fails to develop correctly during the third week of pregnancy. The most serious and most common form of this disability is an open lesion (known as a myelomenigocele) on the child's back in which nerves are exposed. The baby literally has an open spine. Because the nerves are often exposed at birth or covered with only a thin membrane sac, they can be easily damaged or infected. Spinal fluid may also be leaking from the wound.[1]

Spina bifida causes disability. The spinal cord damage will cause at least some loss of muscle strength in the lower body. The victim may also lose feeling in his legs and feet and have bowel and bladder incontinence. At least 70 percent of babies with spina bifida develop hydrocephalus, a swelling of the brain caused by a build-up of spinal fluid.

Spina bifida affects every baby differently. Some learn to walk with the help of assistance devices such as braces. Others experience the loss of all movement in their lower body and will always move through life in a wheelchair. Some children experience a degree of mental retardation, while others possess normal intelligence.

Until very recently most children with spina bifida died

soon after birth. The opening on the back was most often not closed and many times doctors and parents assumed their child would have severe mental retardation. Meningitis and infections often brought a quick death or a life of total confinement and severe retardation.

But today the future is bright for children with spina bifida. Doctors like David McLone and James T. Brown at Children's Memorial Hospital in Chicago send many spina bifida children home to lead near normal lives.[2] Drs. McLone and Brown give aggressive treatment to every child referred to their clinic. No patient is turned away because someone has predicted a low quality of life.

Drs. McLone and Brown do not think anyone can accurately assess any child's chances for survival and development at birth. They have also found that in some cases surgery increases the child's motor function. Drs. McLone and Brown use a team approach with each child. Working with neurosurgeons, pediatricians, neurologists, psychologists and social workers they begin work with each child as early as twenty-four hours after birth. Often surgery is needed. During a delicate operation they try to reconstruct the child's badly formed spinal cord. If hydrocephalus develops after the operation, a shunt is put in place to relieve the pressure of fluid on the child's brain. A team of doctors then carefully monitors the baby's progress and develops therapy programs or prepares for surgery that will be necessary in the future.

In 1981 the doctors provided the results of 100 patients who had been treated at the hospital's clinic. All of these children were aggressively treated. The results were dramatic. Out of the original group of 100, eighty children were progressing and developing well in their situation.

The doctors found that the presence of the back lesion has nothing to do with reduced intelligence. Even the presence of brain swelling did not reduce the child's intellect as long as no infection developed in the central nervous system. If an infection did develop, the chances were great that the baby's

IQ would be decreased. They also found that infections were much less likely to develop if the back lesion had been quickly closed surgically. The key words here are quick action. The doctors found that the child's condition and chances for future development greatly depended on how quickly parents and doctors acted to close the back opening and to prevent infection.

Suzy Mace is one child who was treated at the Chicago clinic. In a *Newsweek* article, her parents told how doctors at the hospital where she was born left them "with the feeling that she's be better off dead than alive." But Suzy was quickly referred to the Chicago hospital and Dr. McLone's team took action. At five years of age Suzy likes to ride her tricycle and sing the alphabet song. Her mother says she is determined to try and walk without her braces. In her mother's own words, "She's a joy."

New equipment is being designed to deal with the practical problems that spina bifida can bring. A new type of brace that uses springs to propel a child's legs with each step is being tested. In the past, lack of bladder control has been a problem and often an embarassment to spina bifida patients. Many times an external pouch was used to hold urine. Now children are learning to use special catheters which require no external devices. Also in the developmental stages is a pacemaker that would regulate the bladder.[3]

Doctors and researchers in Great Britain are also working to prevent spina bifida. Recent studies in that country have shown that spina bifida may be due to a vitamin deficiency, a lack of folic acid in the pregnant woman. Women are now being given special vitamin supplements before and during pregnancy to prevent the occurrence of spina bifida in their unborn children. One study provided the supplements to a group of pregnant women who already had one child with spina bifida. Usually the rate of recurrence for a spina bifida child is five percent. But in this case only one child was born with spina bifida instead of the eight or nine that normally would have been born with spina bifida. In a group of pregnant women where no supplement was given thirteen or five percent of the children, were born with spina bifida.[4]

Despite all these advances, some doctors continue to prescribe nontreatment for babies with spina bifida. In some British hospitals children are routinely selected for nontreatment. What happens to them? Dr. R. B. Zachary wrote in the *British Medical Journal* of his discovery that one hundred percent of the children selected for nontreatment had died—but not of spina bifida. They died because they were given powerful sedatives that made them sleepy and unresponsive. They did not demand food. In short, they were starved to death.

Another British pediatrician who had treated hundreds of children with spina bifida wrote about his own method of killing some of them:

> I offer the baby careful and loving nursing, water sufficient to satisfy thirst, and increasing doses of sedative. A few days after the baby has died I call offering a date for the parents to come and see me . . . when we can gently review what has happened and questions can be asked and answered.[5]

All this is very "kind and compassionate" on the doctor's part, but the fact remains that he helped kill a baby that probably had every chance for life.

American doctors are much more hesitant to talk about infanticide of spina bifida children, but we know of one case that came to public attention in Illinois. Thanks to prompt treatment and adoption by loving parents this little boy is now showing normal intelligence and standing with the help of a walker.

I cite this somewhat technical information on spina bifida for a purpose. The promising research being done on spina bifida shows how medicine can make great progress when we seek to treat the disease instead of simply killing the baby that has the disease. Thirty years ago spina bifida was looked upon as a hopeless condition. No one understood its causes and everyone believed that it signaled severe mental retardation and physical handicap. Yet today we realize many children are not mentally affected and that serious physical handicaps can often be lessened by prompt medical attention. We are coming closer every day to a real cure for this condition. But this kind of work can only be done when there is an attitude of respect for life.

Dr. McLone and his colleagues work hard to treat *every* child brought to them because they believe every child should have a chance. They realized they could not make "quality of life" judgments abut the children they treated. Because of their attitude they have improved the quality of those children's lives and made medical discoveries that will help thousands of children in the future.

We must reject this planned destruction of newborn lives because someone places his own standards of perfection on on their lives. Let us instead follow the example of Dr. Zachary in England.

Under no circumstances would I administer drugs to cause the death of a child. There is no doubt that those who are severely affected at birth will continue to be severely handicapped. But I conceive it to be my duty to overcome the handicap as much as possible and to achieve the maximum development of their potential in as many aspects of life as possible—physical, emotional, recreational and vocational.[6]

TEN

Infanticide
and Nazi Germany

R ECENT HISTORY HAS A LESSON to teach us about infanticide. In America today babies who can live are being "allowed to die" because someone thinks their life isn't worth living. Exactly the same type of killing took place in Nazi Germany long before any Jews were exterminated. Children, the mentally handicapped, the insane, and the merely uncooperative were killed because doctors in the Nazi Reich believed these peoples' lives were devoid of value.

The Nazi experience has several frightening parallels to what is happening in our own country. Mass extermination of Jews and other aliens did not happen in a vacuum. Long before the actual killing, a comprehensive propaganda campaign helped convince the medical profession and the German public that the mentally and physically handicapped deserved to die. School children were fed this line in their text books. The subject of sterilization and euthanasia for mental patients was discussed at doctors' meetings.[1] This propaganda set the stage for the systematic destruction of all who were a hindrance to the Nazi Reich.

Dr. Leo Alexander, an observer at the Nuremberg trials has written eloquently about the small beginnings of the Nazi holocaust.

Whatever proportions these crimes finally assumed, it became evident to all who investigated them that they had started from small beginnings. The beginnings at first were merely a subtle shift in emphasis on the basic attitude of physicians. It started with the acceptance of the attitude . . . that there is such a thing as life not worthy to be lived.[2]

It began with a shift in world view. In our own country today we see that same shift in attitude. We see the pro-infanticide propaganda in the form of medical journal articles and commentaries. We see some of the most highly educated and well-respected doctors in our nation telling us that some human lives are "devoid of value." Think of Dr. Singer's commentary in *Pediatrics* comparing newborn infant children to dogs and pigs.

That same shift in attitudes that preceded the Nazi holocaust is taking root in our own culture today. We have seen the first steps in the deadly progression—the step from killing unborn children to killing handicapped newborn babies. We have no reason to believe it will end here.

We would do well to remember how far the quality of life attitude went in Nazi Germany. Not only were millions of Jews and dissidents killed but gruesome experiments and tortures were performed on captured men, women, and children. New methods for sterilization and castration were tested on concentration camp inmates and prisoners of war. Children were used to test new methods of killing. Human beings were killed, dissected and their brains shipped to German doctors for research and examination. Human life was devoid of all intrinsic value in Nazi Germany. It all began with the idea that some lives are not worthy to be lived.

We have not seen these atrocities in our own nation, but have we really any reason to believe that it won't happen here if we continue on the same course? We have some of the evidence already. What makes us think that we too will not continue on the slippery slide toward death?

Nazis manipulated language to hide what they were doing—just as we do with infanticide. The Nazis used elaborate means to conceal the truth of what was happening to the sick and handicapped. "The Charitable Transport Company for the Sick" was the name given to the bus company that carried the prisoners to their executioners. A special agency set up to handle the systematic killing of children was labelled the "Realm's Committee for Scientific Approach to Severe Illness Due to Heredity and Constitution." The "Charitable Foundation for Institutional Care" was the name given to the government organization that collected the money to pay for the killings from family and relatives of the victim.

The words "infanticide" and "euthanasia" were never used even though the German people knew the special vans in their street were coming to take the people to be gassed. Think of our own manipulation of words. The unborn child is a "product of conception." Abortion is merely the "termination of a pregnancy." Refusing lifesaving surgery for a newborn baby is "letting nature take its course." Starving a handicapped infant to death "is the most loving thing to do." In the Infant Doe case, Judge John Baker ruled that not to treat is a form of treatment.

Like the Nazis, we have manipulated our words to hide the reality of what we are doing. Somehow we think that changing the words will soften the harsh reality of the truth.

It is very easy for us to separate ourselves from the people who committed such crimes. We imagine that they must have been butchers, incapable of love or compassion. We wonder how human beings could have committed such horrible acts.

But the Nazis were human beings like us. They were more similar to us than we like to admit. The doctors who organized and operated the euthanasia program for mental patients in Germany were men who had dedicated their lives to helping the mentally and physically sick. They had opened hospitals, pioneered cures for crippling diseases and achieved for the German medical profession an outstanding reputation.

Dr. Max de Crinis was a professor of psychiatry at Berlin University and director of psychiatry at one of the best hospitals in Europe. He had done extensive work on brain malfunctions and epilepsy. He was concerned about the interactions of body and mind in mental disorders. He had spent his life working to cure the mentally ill. Yet Dr. de Crinis pioneered the euthanasia and infanticide programs in Nazi Germany. He often inspected the shower-like gas chambers and witnessed the murder of adults and children. Dr. de Crinis personally arranged for a thirteen-year-old boy from his own department in the hospital to be sent to a death camp. The boy was mildly affected with Down's Syndrome.[3]

Dr. de Crinis was only one of the outstanding, reputable, well-known German psychiatrists who personally arranged for the murders of thousands of mentally handicapped citizens. The same doctors who had cared for German society's most helpless citizens supervised infants and children being deliberately starved to death. They used adults and children for gruesome human experiments and vivisection.

Today doctors committing infanticide are some of the finest in the medical profession. We expect that when evil happens it will jump out at us. We will easily recognize it and identify evildoers. But that is not the case today, just as it was not the case in Nazi Germany. The most horrible crimes were performed by the most reputable citizens. Infanticide and euthanasia were "hidden crimes" in Nazi Germany. They took place quietly, in clean, orderly sterile hospitals. They were committed by the very people in society to whom the Germans entrusted their sick and handicapped citizens. Is it any different today when outstanding doctors in some of the most prestigious hospitals in the country write the words "Do Not Feed" on the chart of a baby with Down's Syndrome, and then leave that child to starve to death?

ELEVEN

Where Do We Go From Here?

WE NEED TO BE CLEAR about a few points. First, there are "hard cases" where the price we pay for life is very high. But we must also maintain the principle that death is never a solution. Let me explain.

It would be a lie to say that there are no "hard cases" involving handicapped children and adults. In some cases a child is uncontrollable, husbands and wives have divorced because of the strain of raising this child, and other family members have developed emotional problems because of the added stress in the family. Some children require twenty-four hour attention from specially trained attendants. Sometimes a child is destructive and unable to communicate his needs. Some cannot attend to their own bodily needs. Parents and families can be faced with an intense and time consuming care routine that will continue for the life of their child.

But what do we say in the midst of these hard cases? Do we agree with so many around us who say that death is the best choice? No. We must firmly reject the idea that killing is compassionate. Killing the child is never the solution. But for now we must realize that the real need is for life-giving solutions. We must choose life or death. We live in a society where human life is cheap. We have abandoned a world view that affirms the dignity and worth of every human life. All around us we hear that death is the best answer for all those who do not measure up to our standards of perfection.

But can we really say that there is a person so disabled that they cannot respond to love. However limited the abilities might be, can we honestly say that this child cannot feel a touch given in love or cannot respond to a gentle word spoken to them?

As Christians we must completely reject the utilitarian thinking that says death is best. Our energies should be directed instead toward helping that child to fulfill whatever potential he has to grow and learn. We should also help the family with the many needs it will have in the course of raising a disabled member.

Often we are tempted to look at a particular situation and say that it would have been better if the child had never been born. Of course there are situations where life would have been easier for the family if the child had not been born. But do we mean that we should have killed that child at birth? How would we have made that decision at birth? How would we have made this kind of killing legal under our laws?

The fact is that the child was born and that child reflects the image of God in some unique way. That image may be completely hidden from view. There may be tremendous emotional and physical problems to be solved for the family. But that is exactly the course we should take—devoting our time, energy and money to helping everyone live the best possible life in that situation. For a Christian, killing is never compassionate.

But it is not enough to stop there. If we say that handicapped children deserve every protection we can offer them, we must also be prepared to share the responsibility of caring for them as children and as adults. In the pro-life movement there is a popular slogan—Being Pro-Life Means More Than Being Anti-Abortion. That means that fighting against abortion also means caring for children and for the mothers who might otherwise seek an abortion. In the same way, we must oppose infanticide and also work just as hard to help the children and families after they are born.

Our government has a responsibility to care for the truly needy in society. Many handicapped citizens clearly fall into this category. But programs to provide education and services for handicapped citizens are inadequate, and many of them are being cut back by state and federal governments.

These programs need protection. I have some personal experience about how it can work. Our own little boy has attended a Parent-Infant Program weekly since he was three months old. The program was a wonderful help for Will and myself. I learned the basics of child development and the many ways I could stimulate Will's development. We had the undivided attention of a therapist once a week and complete testing services for Will's sight and hearing whenever they were needed. All of this came to us free of charge because the program was state and federally funded.

But every year this program is threatened with a funding cut. The year Will and I took the class, the program survived federal and state budget cuts only because concerned parents and friends launched a determined letter writing campaign to public officials.

Education and public awareness are also very important. One of the first emotions parents feel at the birth of a handicapped child is a sense of isolation. They often feel like they are the only people to ever face such a problem. Many times they have never heard of their child's condition. Often doctors themselves are ignorant or uninformed of the latest developments in the treatment of the disability.

In the last several years parent support groups and educational organizations have been forming to pass on information and support to families. All of us are in a position to pass on this kind of information to friends and families who need help.

It is difficult to overestimate the importance of the handicap advocacy organizations. Many times just knowing that there are people who can help and who share the experience themselves can make the difference between a family keeping their child instead of putting him in a special home.

In our area a local group called the Down's Development Council has put together a "New Parents Packet" which includes educational information about Down's Syndrome as well as several touching stories from parents and a list of important names, addresses, and organizations. From this packet we learned that Will was eligible to be enrolled in the Parent-Infant Program in our area. We also received the most current information about our son's condition and began to understand all we could do to help his growth and development.

But there's more to give than support for funding for special programs and support for local associations. We can share ourselves with parents and handicapped children.

There is much we can do; it does not always take an expert to help a handicapped child and his family. We can do much just by spending a few hours a week helping to provide extra stimulation and new learning experiences for a child. Parents need help teaching or training their child. Devoting a few of your hours a week can give them a much-needed break from a tiring day.

We have found that teaching Will requires extra imagination and patience. He needs much more stimulation and repetition to learn things that may be easy for other children. But he does learn and the rewards of seeing him master a new task just cannot be measured. These are rewards that our friends share too as they spend time with Will.

How many women return to work after the children are grown to fill the empty hours? Why not devote some of that available time to helping a special child? Perhaps you could make a teaching toy or sew up a special kind of doll that helps children learn how to use zippers, snaps and buttons. The ideas are endless once we realize that we can really make a difference in a child's life.

There is so much wasted talent in our church pews. The idea of ministering to the handicapped is a novel idea in many churches. Of all the institutions in our society that should help share the responsibility, churches should be the first to give help.

The church made a big difference for us when Will was born. Everyone pitched in: meals were cooked, rooms were painted, and chores were all done by our friends at church. Chris and Al Gaspar, church members and neighbors, volunteered to help babysit several mornings a week while I spent time at the library writing this book. Other friends at church were just there to listen and give us both a shoulder to cry on when the tears came. Whenever an article or television show about Down's Syndrome appeared they brought the clippings or gave us notes they had taken during the broadcast. There were many difficult times that first year. But we always felt the love and support of our church. With Bill's long hours at work and my writing obligations, I do not know how we would have managed without the love and care of our friends.

Unhappily, not every case is like our own. I know of a family with a severely retarded child who has tried many times to destroy himself. His parents had been forced to place him in a state facility that was not the best. It was a terrible situation for this family. Both mother and father were dying emotionally and spiritually.

They had wanted to keep their son at home but they could not do so without help. Sadly, they could get no help from their church. They had mentioned their needs several times at prayer meetings with other church members. The response had always been that they would pray, but nothing more.

This family needed so much more. They needed people who would give their time each week to babysit and let husband and wife have time alone together. They needed friends who would listen to them when they shared their fears and frustrations. As the years went by, their marriage and their lives began to dissolve. Let's face it, this was not a neat and tidy situation. Anyone who would get "involved" would get their hands dirty and possibly get very little in tangible returns. But what they would have gotten is the satisfaction of knowing they had helped save a family.

It is not enough to tell a parent that you must choose life and then walk away. Our words mean nothing if we do not back them up with loving support for that family.

Not long after Will was born, my husband and I had dinner with a young couple. Our pediatrician had asked us to talk to them about their new baby. Their child had been born with a severe handicap. After three weeks in the intensive care unit he had been released. His young mother was not even able to leave the house because of the special care her baby needed. The doctors could not give them any hope for the future. In all likelihood, they were looking at a lifetime of constant care for their child.

The young woman, who loves Christ, did not need to be told to choose life. She and her husband dearly loved their baby and were willing to do anything for him. She needed someone to come and visit during the long hours of the week. She needed someone to learn how to use the machines they had for the baby so she could leave the house for a few hours, even if it was just to go to the grocery store. She needed a friend to listen when the harsh realities of her baby's condition brought tears and depression.

We cannot lightly say to parents or society "choose life." In some situations, making that choice will bring years of sacrifice and pain. We must be there to ease that pain and share the burden with them. In so many situations, God can use us to prevent a family from shattering and a heart from breaking.

Let's put things in perspective. Isn't it time we stopped spending our free hours at so many church potlucks and Christian exercise classes? In our families, our neighborhoods, our churches, there are children and families who need our help. We live in a society where human life is cheap. If we speak out against the utilitarian killing of newborn children, we must also stand ready to help that child reflect the image of a loving creator.

All of these suggestions for helping may seem like very small things to do to make a dent in such a big problem. But we must remember that small beginnings often produce the greatest results. How can we measure the importance of bringing love and meaning to just one person's life? Each of us, in some small way, can help bring that extra care to someone's life.

In Closing

Wouldn't it be nice if we did not have to discuss infanticide? Wouldn't it be wonderful if all parents loved their children and handicapped infants received *special* care because of their special needs?

Unfortunately, infanticide is a fact in the United States. Some newborn babies are denied routine treatment, some literally starved to death, because someone thinks their life is not worth living.

The time for discussion is past. Christians and all concerned citizens must join in the fight to protect helpless human beings. I often hear Christians say that it takes a special calling to be involved in the pro-life movement—that not every believer is called to fight against these evils. It is true, not every Christian can write or speak on these issues. But every believer has a part to play in the fight. Infanticide, just like abortion, is not a "single issue." It is a question of human life. And as Francis Schaeffer has said, "If we cannot take a stand for life, when will we take a stand?"

Notes

Chapter Two
Infanticide: Down the Slippery Slope

1. "Declaratory Judgment in the Matter of the Treatment and Care of Infant Doe," Judge John G. Baker, Monroe County Circuit Court, April 12, 1982.
2. Anne Bannon, M.D., "The Case of the Bloomington Baby," *Human Life Review,* Fall 1982, vol. viii, no. 4, p. 68.
3. Mary Arnold, "Some Doctors Feel They Have the Right to Kill Defective Children," *Catholic Twin Circle,* August 23, 1983, p. 4.
4. Americans United for Life, press release, Dec. 5, 1983.
5. Joseph Fletcher, "Infanticide and the Ethics of Loving Concern," in *Infanticide and the Value of Life,* Marvin Kohl, ed. 1978, p. 17.
6. Milton Heifetz and Charles Mangel, *The Right to Die,* 1975, p. 51.
7. "A New Medical Ethic," *California Medicine,* Vol 113, No. 3, September 1970, pp. 67-68.
8. Peter Singer, "Sanctity of Life, Quality of Life," *Pediatrics,* vol. 72, no. 1, 1983, p. 18.
9. Raymond S. Duff and A.G.M. Campbell, "Moral and Ethical Dilemmas in the Special Care Nursery," *New England Journal of Medicine,* vol. 289, no. 17, October 25, 1973, pp. 890-94.
10. Shaw, Randolph, and Manard, "Ethical Issues in Pediatric Surgery: A National Survey of Pediatricians and Pediatric Surgeons," 60 *Pediatrics* 588 (1977). See also *Mental Retardation,* "Physicians' Attitudes toward Discretionary Medical Treatment of Down's Syndrome Infants," April 1980, pp. 79-81.

Chapter Three
"Complexity" and Other Issues

1. C. Everett Koop, M.D., "The Seriously Ill Child: Supporting the Patient and the Family," *Death, Dying and Euthanasia,* Dennis J. Horan and David Mall, eds. (University Publications of America, 1977), p. 547.
2. Transcript of April 13, 1982, in regards to Infant Doe, a child in need of services, No. JU-8204-038A (Circuit Court of Monroe County, Indiana).

Chapter Four
Treatment vs. Nontreatment

1. C. Everett Koop, M.D., and Francis A. Schaeffer, *Whatever Happened to the Human Race?* (book and film) (Old Tappan, New Jersey: Fleming H. Revell Co., 1979).
2. Anonymous, *The Lancet,* November 24, 1979, p. 1123.
3. C. Everett Koop, "Ethical and Surgical Considerations in the Care of Newborns with Congenital Anomalies," *Infanticide and the Handicapped Newborn,* (Provo, Utah: Brigham Young Univ. Press, 1982), p. 96.
4. Koop, *Infanticide and the Handicapped Newborn,* p. 101.
5. *Ibid.*

Chapter Five
Parents' Rights

1. Duff and Campbell, Op. cit.
2. *Ibid.*

Chapter Six
The Law and Infanticide

1. John A. Robertson, "Legal Aspects of Withholding Medical Treatment from Handicapped Children," *Infanticide and the Handicapped Newborn,* p. 22.
2. *Maine Medical Center v. Houle,* No. 14-145. Superior Court, Cumberland, Maine, dec. Feb. 14, 1974. Quoted in Robertson, *Infanticide and the Handicapped Newborn,* p. 24.
3. Dennis J. Horan and Steven R. Valentine, "The Doctor's Dilemma," *Infanticide and the Handicapped Newborn,* p. 41.
4. 106 Cal. App. 3d 811, 165, Cal. Rptr. 477(1980)
5. *National Review,* Sept. 2, 1983, p. 1069.

Chapter Eight
Down's Syndrome

1. One of the best books available on Down's Syndrome is *Down's Syndrome—Growing and Learning,* Siegfried M. Pueschel, Claire Canning, et al., eds. (Kansas City, Kansas: Andrews and McMeel Co., 1978).

Chapter Nine
Spina Bifida

1. For further information, write Spina Bifida Association of America, 3435 Dearborn, Suite 319, Chicago, Illinois 60604, (312) 663-1562.
2. See James T. Brown and David McLone "Treatment Choices for the

Infant with Meningomyelocele," *Infanticide and the Handicapped New-born,* p. 69-75.

3. "Saving Spina Bifida Babies," *Newsweek,* Nov. 15, 1982.
4. R.W. Smithells, "Possible Prevention of Neural-Tube Defects by Periconceptional Vitamin Supplementation," *The Lancet,* Feb. 16, 1980, pp. 339-40.
5. A   123-24.
6.